UNCITY,
lean

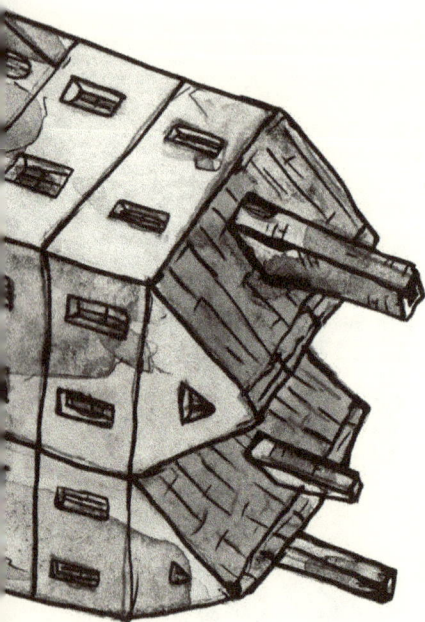

UNCITY, lean

POEMS

Michael Cooper

Alternating Current Press
Boulder, Colorado

Uncity, Lean
Michael Cooper
©2021 Alternating Current Press

Alternating Current
Boulder, Colorado
press.alternatingcurrentarts.com

ISBN: 978-1-946580-22-1
First Edition: February 2021

To Kyle: It should have been I who succumbed to the landscape that we were raised in. Thank you for being there when I am alone, brother, for when things sting, keen, or shine, and always grinning. I will see you on the trail again, all smiles.

To Chad: Thank you for helping me heal my mind when I was wounded and at my least reasonable, for giving me my words back through surrealism. Thank you for traveling through this time with me; I could not have been an easy companion, in all that unquiet.

TABLE of CONTENTS

A first step towards reawakening respect
for your inner life may be to become
aware of your private collage of
dead names you have for your inner life.
          —John O' Donohue, *Eternal Echoes*

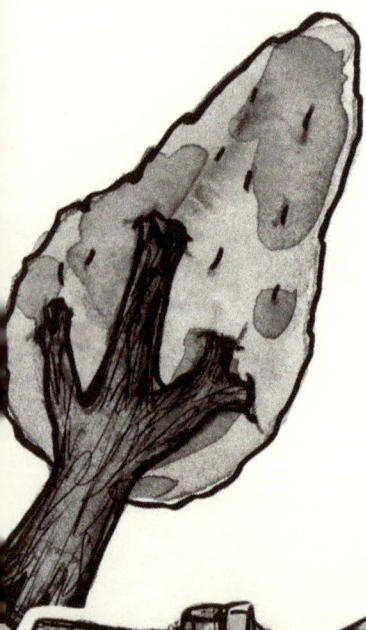

MIDNIGHT
FIRETRUCK

welcome to our gray shag
carpet our screams of hallway
our overflow

I.

Just poke a finger through to breathe again. I live for my first 5 years rolling with my younger cousin inside a Firestone tire. Uncle hand-loads shells with rock salt. Hide-and-seek only hurts when Papa isn't too drunk to outrun us, the muzzle of his weapon flashing green-white.

2.

We hide in the unfinished houses of the suburban tracts as unfinished people. We share a pickup truck's back seat with his gunrack and his new wife Mary's bruised face. Mary will never replace my aunt: but we all "fall down the stairs" just the same way she did in these bored-wood frameworks. She is just like all of us who wait for the drywall and running water to install itself within us. *The surrounding poems were meant to escape this somehow.*

3.

I still can feel the long gray-haired
cat—watch the memories of
myself torture her in the too-hot
shower or swung by her arms—I
hear her crying now, and I feel it
inside myself, an endless sorry.

                        This mythos made of youth that

abuse goes nowhere.

                        It is only too easy to lose myself as an
academic, to sit and watch as "hegemony" shifts—
and as power
                        redistributes: so does powerlessness

                        and the downward thrill-spill of

aggression: just watch.

Or poke a finger into his new
wife's raw face.

                        Stare.

4.

Mary will find the harpoon for you if she feels you weak enough, and despite any compassion you may lend her. "You will always be

here: I'll show you how pain is easily and unequally

redistributed." *It is easier to lose myself in the urban-scape.* This is the reason I know all of the breaks in chain-link and razor-wire fences on the 10 freeway overpasses, from Banning to East Los.

5.

Cousin and I can't unleap this overpass. *Veracity matters: it makes it so much easier for me to shelter behind indecipherable images.* Stare down the shadow of traffic, follow this storm to its pile of bones. Each of us a cage, feet covered in off-white flecked excrement.

Between.

6.

We are made hungry, but first, inhale the ivory fungus that claws the split-top of the butterloaf bread, before cousin closes the bag, and we turn away in disgust. Run upstairs to become the rooftop-scarecrow burn among unstartled pidgins. Each of us cage.

This decimal is.

7.

The midnight firetruck stalls outside the 99-cent discount. Every convergent hour, like cross-eyed Mary. *What apricot?* Relentless thrum of the mute and handicap, the Red Bull spins.

8.

We run away to live in a discotheque kept so cold the
subwoofers bleed. Saran Wrap over his mouth, he sur-
renders. Fire, this impenetrable. The nervous chap-
erone makes eye contact with us, pantomimes slitting
our throats, "go home go home," we are home

where the black widow stumbles under her burden
across the webbed marble shower, grooms the talk of
the day through her threads, guards us, her wriggling
orbs.

9.

Our Sunday Football discipline of linemen in the crush grows homicidally ridiculous. Spit pit, un-mouthed the savorer. Horn Architecture, this gift of mating rams. We plastic-wrap the toy firetruck, plunge it to fathom the tub.

10.

The fish all drown upstairs, the people's gills empty.
So, I set the last pidgin free. The languages of cage and
the infant. Poke a finger through to breathe again.

II.

How many times did my uncle die in my imagination:
choking on the apricot pit, his head in Saran Wrap
staring like leftovers, gutted on the antlers of his cap-
tured and mounted prey: how he taught me this.

How he unleapt that overpass; he pushes from a place
between his own legs.

How the hand-loaded shotgun turns into the cold-
sawn-barrel piping my lips.

How my inside-out body spreads denial of a bruise,
and the denial of these bruises I have given.

I am all of these threshing bodies, salmon left to drown
unmated in our unfilled bathtub—nowhere to fly but
the bathroom floor.

12.

I welcome you to feel our shag carpet, our screams of hallway: overflow of ashtray lungs. Fist-for-hello, go, sing the midnight firetruck of the good-life among these 99-cent stores.

AS IDIOT CHILDREN

those who grow
the architecture of horns and those who grow within
it

Playground I

I am here floating above the tarmac with my hands tucked in the pockets of my unbuttoned windbreaker that I've flipped up over my head—my arms spread it like batwings letting the wind catch and lift me—I believe I am a starship—unsheathed and sprinting away from this windbreaker—to let the rain into me.

Leap from the swings, the imperial gray fever let me drop into the cradled gravity of the sandbox—give myself over to what leaps into those aviator goggles—into what cockpits!

Playground II

The Stormtrooper's muzzle spits—and me in my scarf
and mittens. They gather around us like plastic-
limbed action figures as I square off with some other
boy to Rochambeau over who has the more inattentive
father—each nerve ending something more than just
some camera smarting—we escape the gravity of this
together in that moment we hang in space before our
butts touch down just past the pit dug by the kicking
feet of the other leaping swingers that fell to earth be-
fore us.

Playground III

We children writhe up from the hair in our horns—
rise from the home, the spike, the body, a mask the
lash of this whipline self that threshes behind it.

These things voiced—a falling tower crushes—we so
permeable that act carefree: are powerful in what

we believe—sing song kick him in the penis kick him
in the—ears whetted and asses stinging—my nose
runs snuffled onto sleeve cuffs—then the sun breaks
open the sky—runs its fingers through our unlaven-
dered hair—smelling of gunstock oil and Jesus can-
dles.

Every Love Song I Sing to Myself

Slips backward into the child
I was   there   listening
my shoes unfilled but I knew
        the tune   of lonely prey
                cannot feel each cry
                of the eaten alive.
What possible mechanism relieves
                the pain of Papa
                        the loitering
                night watchmen from   the apparition
                        of his son   himself
                an abandoned son   the love
                of brothers falling   through
the bomb bay secrets of
        the cloistered sisters at   the loom
    every love song slips back into the child I was   listen
to the modem's heartbeat for some comfort.

Art Lesson I

Unwrap the crayons one by one to lose the color of their names. Cut-crush them with a boxcutter blade, then heat small amounts on a spoon. Do this without adult super vision. Drip them down on the unaccustomed eyes of these page-bound images.

Dream of an anglerfish lost among salmon's leap, the three-horned rhinosauri charging, the Stormtroopers on their overwatch and endlessly waiting to

shoot at the unmoving enemy. Lost in my haiku about snow and deer, which I never left the city to see. The widow-dream of mother's long blue-black hair, spiraling up vertically into the vortex of my first defensive horn.

History Lesson I

Never forget that my breath starts at my feet and out through my mouthpiece, and the air outside me and inside me collapses to a single always-moving

medium I use to speak with the dead columns of soldiers, heroes slumping back from the Russian steppes and no leader among them. The rags around their feet are our stomachs, and the flags they wave are we children.

I am incapable of feeling pain. There is no me to feel the cold, the black bloody feet unwrapping themselves into their own desperate unguent—there is no me to contain this. There must be some other way to be.

The steel mill died, and then the speedway, and then the airbase, and then the vineyard unwrapped her coiled hair into the picketed tract homes poured asphalt into her mouth, and in every remaining crack weeds waited for when they would decide it was our time to go.

History Lesson II

These teeth in my hip pocket, whose are they. When I endure the cold-jacketless-morning, do I look to winter or the desert as mother. Why do adults require such loyalties from us? What was this first nest I lived in, but this thorned night made up of loyalties, the absence of

security: the threat of falling is what keeps the successful warbler fledglings flying. Because—no one to greet my fall: the leaves turn to face the sun, everything but us remembers.

A Prayer for the Horned-Ones I

This is not the sunrise on ab-
normality, I/we are anomaly
ubiquitous but
aware how this urban-scape ate at all of us. The great
curl of amber street
lights overhang those street-side late-night walkers desperate
for a hug, a smile, for the most dangerous thing:
the atavism of their perceived
normalcy. Each of the us is buried

terracotta
soldiers dripping
condensation

from their eyes, dress right dress [how we are
forgotten—cotton wifebeaters ripped open] a launch
code in each breast pocket, a twin set of latchkeys,

and some deadman's switch
           nicking the back of our legs, that's how
we
will learn to agree.

A Prayer for the Horned-Ones II

Trucks crush the pottery
      left out on the corner of E Street,
      their tires roll—shoot clay
      in the roll-up garage down the block,
      the young man
      gets
his 2nd facial tattoo, 2 tears

"how to make a homemade prison
      tattoo
machine requires a few basic parts . . . an old Walk-
man,
      a guitar string, an ink
pen,   an eraser, a tooth-
brush, and some tape
        hold it all together."

This is the communion of each new fragment: "there
are many [bodies], but this one is mine. My [body] is
my best friend, it is
my life. Without me
my [body] is useless, without my [body] I am useless."
This is my

body. This is my tooth. These are my pains, and the
pains I have given you.

O Mother Night, O Widow, passed love, little weaver of our world—wash out the sun with your tender mercy—birth this absence of light, give us something, we thousand, clamber to eat.

Playground IV

Children, what fed me to them? What hung me out like wet-lost sheets on their barbed-wire clothesline, what grail

did I drink the gas from that spilt me from my container. Am I siphoned milk? Who robbed me from the udder—what unsheathed me and left me on the snow tracing bloodlines of my country's enemies in the tundra?

Art Lesson II

There is only one being
more hideous and pathetic than the deeply
submerged angler-
fish, luring other fish with its curled
bioluminescent antler
close enough
for it to consume them, and that is
this being I created in its likeness
out of melted crayon
to bring the other
children closer
to look at me,
so I could pretend
we could be friends.

Playground V

Make sure No-one followed my trail, no ambush was sprung. No, sadly, this is just another game of hide-and-seek played all by myself. That mirror—shrugs, asks

if war is so unpopular why does the young marrow drink it so? We spend our whole lives

preparing for it, preparing the words—we sight down the barrel at the image of a human, squeeze lightly, breathe out fogging, not knowing when the bolt carrier will slam forward, and then—as if by ritual—the weapon cycles, and the decimal place is shifted—at what cost. This is my body, this is your body.

The Classroom Won

Imagine children without a war, at a desk. Imagine their scribbling and their formations. Such plans. I can't imagine what I have already lived.

I can't imagine the 6th graders lining up in drama class to slap the back of my neck with their rulers, the way they broke their wrist hitting me, dripping with their spit.

A Prayer for the Horned-Ones III

We, the abandoned-self history, leapfrog neighbor-hoods from green to green street sign love and misery blurring in vinyl sheets and street lights measuring time by the trees that strobe as we run from whatever it is that is chasing us—time measures the overturned ketchup bottle waiting for the knife to ring in its mouth —broken glass and rock salt entering our skin. The cartridges I hand-loaded and stuffed into my uncle's choke, everything slide action through the projects stubble beards of stubborn plyboard and drywall that grab for the thick plastic sheets like Saran Wrap sta-pled over a home's mouth—this freeway isn't long enough, 230 years of vineyard underneath her arms Mary runs her hands of wet concrete through the thistles winging crickets leap in all directions the head-less coyote sings sleeping and ½-mile away his jaw-bone stuck in a Bobcat's tread in front of the freshly-built Walmart. Watch me poke a finger through to

breathe again.

We Continue to Dream,
Onward into the Dawn

tied to our truant poles by our *long-*
tailed school shirts.

They didn't bother to move
  the headstone from my desk the Nightman's truncheon
big
      as a slamming tailgate   as he stalked crossing
          over his rails   I watch him piss
into the ballast his wristwatch
loose-banded glint dangling
from the sleeve of his black service
                uniform.   I dug upward all night
  just to see Papa   trace the engine's amber yawn
against the cowling of the sky
that pulls the cattle cars braying
past the   plyboard cruciforms
to the split-
hung midnight of the slaughterhouses.

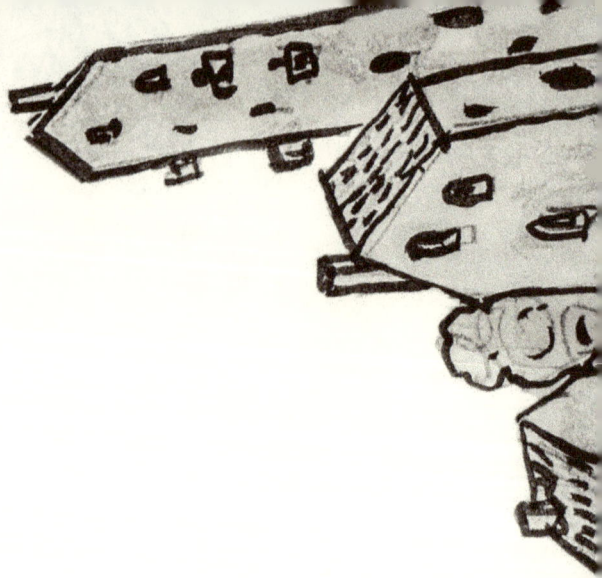

UNCITY

because
it is too easy to say this assemblage
is made of us
as we and our communities
are dismantled

The Return Commute through the Street-Fight I Am Transmuted to You through Sound

i.

my hands on your waist your tears inches from my lips
I would recognize you anywhere in any form this fall-
ing into this family this movement of the sun behind
your head and the faces of our children on your loom
we have slain the unicorn evils with each hand-fasting
made friends with the dark

we have lain among the forms of the world and
screamed the songs of longing how could I leave you

ii.

how could I leave you among these blind working peo-
ple

On my way home I see two groups of homeless people
fighting over a "stolen" bicycle they throw rocks at
each other wrapped in the light that springs from
dropped storefront windows the mannequins on dis-
play leering through the broken teeth of the frame

as the ramshackle-defeated group speeds away the vic-
torious one begins to scream at one another they tear
at each other's faces it seems pointless to me

as I get into my car and drive off but to them access to
a bicycle is a promotion: the freedom to

collect cans and plastic stuffed into plastic bags that
bow handlebars and outrider pegs

I watch them stand on the pedals to move their heavy
loads into the passing day ruled by the overlooking
saints

locked in you I remember the crippled man's crutch
that I stole

Trombone—I put you to my lips and blow—O imper-
fect embouchure my lips pressed to yours this melody
mine as I move the telescoping slide in and out to fol-
low some thread I've found.

iii.

some thread I've found
and I begin to weave you
we are reborn in waves and arm motions until I pull
myself into a ball wrapped around you Victrola with
the disconnected speaker—play Igor's *Firebird* suite

feel the pulse of the box while the needle and turntable
heat the grooves into this distorted signal

where we are the lungs and the vibration and the com-
position and the deep movement of the horn sections
and those goddamned strings celebrating return re-
turn this last moment return

I smell your hair on my shoulders that I would find in
my car days later and smile

your passage through my life as touchable as sum
beauty of all landscapes
sunsets
you hold me like an anthem
to fight off the blistered feet the mantra of the bored
fire in the night of those
who would lie down and die
the streetlamps extinguished and I hear the boys stir
and I smile
ready to renew the cycle
and Kyle grins the grin of chains and fences

Our Lives Depend on Knowing
What to Wear, What to Say

they held a fashion show   on the morning of our discovery
of the trombone   mute—I'm in my shower
curtain frock and she   regal in the nets
we use to dredge the lake   stare—at each other
across   the hook-gouged Formica table
as if we   have nothing to say   The milk
in our cereal so cold it leaves ice
beards on the lips of our bowls—Outside our
                    lamb brays at the oncoming
                              mailman
              as if our lives depend on knowing
                    of his approach on the garbage
scow of the sidewalk the wind-hurled prow swings
leeward to run south
        to break up   the slip ice of the catwalk

My Friend Ended Himself the Grass Grows

the black ice weaves itself like leaves
undispersing the light each hydrostat a pre-coded
strategy of capture   each a blade   the stoplight
cameras run out of film long   before

money loses
  its value   a mailroom breach   its sort left to the lichen
among
      the slots   in and out boxes   the people
clumped fungi   pieces of them are hacked off
smaller stalks rise among the waist-
  high grasses   that engulf our sidewalks their letters
lost   his text

  left unanswered I didn't
 know
  Kyle slowly loads the revolver of late night
at my terminal Ascii opens and closes its sideways
mouth the way
  each crowd has its yesses and its no's the umbrellas
bloom in unison to catch water in their beaks

To Make Popular Love Songs Overhead

I watch their beaks move
the Vocoder matches signals predetermined to be melody
I think this is crying
this is to rock myself gently
this is to decode
        to unalienate
the owner of the cock's comb voices stare-jabber
this storefront is theirs
wings mantle over this meal
        To order this meal
my ear is struck by their fist
                        that was a Double Double Animal-
Style Fries well done with a Coke
it is not to be permitted to live
without depriving other beings of their lives
this last squeal
        as the needle goes in and out
        of each suture between you and I
begins with some laceration locomotive—that
comes on to you like daggers
and I caught here with handfuls of coal
        each big-bodied and defenseless I
want you to lay down on my tracks to sleep beautifully
the coordinates of our cage are fixed
in our wet-work
memory banks rear up
I dash my hooves into you
        weave   layers of spurting   coaxial cables
whore each image—

a witness and a defense and my love of parallel
mystery join me at the erasure of our horizon
clutch with fiber-optic cables
      the corrugated aluminum of our shacks ask
am I emulating the correct pitches of your love songs? Or
are the diesel bodies of gods thrumming along
my tracks to make deaf our pleas.

Work in San Bernardina

and then as if pleading before us it opened
we with our shivs to the lamb's belly
we painted our faces told our fortunes in its entrails
is this a wake   Is this
work   The multiple unsorted letters all
    say the same thing strung out
like the radio that lungs 1200 voices that play
the same songs demanded by the same closed-door
committee

 I confuse them—the difference
    between being in my body and using
my body   the threshold of some timeclock
the shock of near death is an awareness of the composite
materials we are made of as if all the laughter
curled inside   this one moment of departure
because even this threshold of work is password-protected

   but our muscles have deeper memory of these
rituals than we do
the trickle-up-politics of predation
lead us
to a chalk outline of a supermarket I
   decode
the mail and inside each envelope is
            a fresh-wrapped commodity
fresh-wrapped in individual for-sale
packaging fresh

The Sleep: The Philosopher,
the Cubicle

am I asleep at work again an individual
for sale
Nietzsche
              strokes the long nose of the horse
they lean
              into the quick wonder of her breathing
unbit
    unbridled unlashed unbearable lightness

am I asleep
                          at work again interrogating
              the petroglyph of boredom
the monitor blinks
    tears from its screen someone must reimagine this
place
as a
                          livable space Black
              Shuck bellows in the hollow grove of

their beaks the cancer
                          slows and sleeps beyond
    their wings of their solar panels that fly under the
fury of the pale

moon a series of photographs illustrate a horse
running herself to death
    the close up of Deerwoman's mascara
running with her eyes green
    bore through the celluloid   am I asleep at
work again

The Sleep: The Foxhole,
the Angel, the Home

    collect the dew from the lens of the fallen long
tongues deep inside their gasmasks imagine being
    asleep at work imagine being
that desperate hand that cranks the air-raid siren the
    gargoyle leans its head back
sweat swept from the sonic assault of its lips to warn of
the inbound
    sleep of work
sleep of work
 !Incoming
The Cherubim their Newtonian masses afire
   scrambled every networked fighter-eye
eye-impugning
    thrust judgment naked into another
and another passerby am I
    asleep at my cubicle again   The omnipresent
vacuum cleaners strain
    but make no sound as we are sucked in

and if we are American
    we are always much too loudly awake
at work
      again warming the last potato over
the transistor tube's buzz or am I jobless
    the structure set us aside am I asleep
on the couch with my wife and the boys watching
      TV the wolf cubs play hide-
and-seek in the dandelions gray tufts blowing
    in the grass spreading lawn to lawn yellow I rub
this one under your chin nuzzle my love—pollen
    marking you yellow
as the sunspots each of us a finger
       reaching into space to shade our eyes lift up
these heads let us unweep

To Some the Highway Is Just a High-Power Rifle

all along it runs
  ubiquitous chain-link fences   each rust
spot their own   fingerprint   we climb up the rungs
      of the tender power
  lines   the earth was just some vehicle for their
work. The way the palm trees behave will make much
      more sense
  when you realize that they are a grass   they network
shed their fronds for aerial antlers that boost
  the cell signal of "the collected good" shot out along
the highways   aimed with the aid of 10x scopes we are
  a diaspora of use.
A voice is the   keen-edged

              instrumentality of I   am broken typewriter
I am a machine ribbon battered
    by broken teeth. We the incomplete
alphabet provided by ancient
  merchants
        clamber up the poles at night among the cranes
and engines of translucent might
        that lift their towers into the sky
I cling to my vestigial
                  naïveté
         even sunset in the foothills is red
the light of the city stoops winged like some ambient
  predator

no tequila could drown   I am strapped up here
among the phone
      lines
soulless   with the long-haul diesels peering through
  this night
 scope of blackened delight

But I Always Thought
That I'd See You Again

black Labrador runs out between the cars
    barely see her as I skid and she
    goes under my bumper the way I like

            to curl around my family and li
sten to them sleep   performing the Mueller maneuver Dr.
        Shoar assesses his victim with profound
    sleep   apnea   judged by the possessions
      of the heart the panting the feral
      start stop cries of *Black Dog* from shivering
speakers   each moment stuck in the throat of   now
       rises like the heat signature off my

   tires pushing the earth away   hold on
covered with my coat she is someone's   I
  carry her home soak-curled and shaking in
          fetal position and half asleep
       I feel Black Shuck clamber down into my
nest   his bones my bones we laugh we laugh we

No "They," We Are All
One Organism Of

      the shared phantom   the shinbone keeps my dogs
barking at the Black & Whites muscle
          cars and little boys filling the loafers
of their pixel-sprung selfie-taking fathers   a still life
     and the half-thawed burrito   in its plastic wrapper
makes up its own disclaimers to dress itself

                         in don't touch
        anything it's all evidence   a typo makes
a text threatening *I'm sleeping*

      with your mom again   the desperate seeking   of
the billboard for your latchkey
                 milked and each waiting
           for their turn with the pneumatic
hammer   I just want to see him on the trail again
                     Kyle's hip
        pocampus as art displayed   the never quite dry
                 splash of cherry-cola on
drywall

The In-N-Out across the Street from Our Bedroom Window

Half-full Coke can
spill rolls across
the In-N-Out
parking lot behind
our second story
backroom apartment
where we force love
between teeth and sheets.

How do you spend
profound moments?
Covered in someone
else's ecstasy.
Crossed palms—cars park
eat, drink, and leave.

She Leaves Me Like

   keyless entry cars leave   into the dewlit sunward wonder
While I wrestle   my inner-Marxist as if life were
          the redistribution of   receipts &
chicken-sandwich wrappers   I know we
           donate   to the roots
      no more lies   we are fed into the ground
   and from us every   vehicle on the road sprouts
  bipinnate
2 x 2   smaller versions   of versions of itself

                leaves
we the speaker a closed-circuit
and 9-volt battery that form
             the home alarm system
hacked & without any senses without
         loved ones to come within us
to set us off
when   the day is done

This, the Real Love Song to the Unknown, I Held a Dying

dog on the day of her job interview

her fishbowl too much
    for me to bear walking by   nothing happens
here
     we hold hands and pretend we are ok like

   the air that hangs between her lungs and mine isn't
poison she
  peers in like quadraphonic sound

    this is the revolution back to now on the
              turntable of the sky
I am kissed by her hand and the heat reddens

  my cheek each of my bus transfers requires a few
more numb senses

 we linger just past the point
    where reconciliation with my parents is possible and
the landmines they planted
    have us repeating their amputated lives
              now

you dear standing there with
    our neighbor's wet fucking dog leaking blood into the carpet
we are
    two Japanese fighting fish

        that stare   at each other   mirrors
                                    floating upside down
in two separate bowls.

Love Bomb and Loving
the Moon on the Lawn

on our backs looking out of the mirror of you
their gray yawn is illusion   only
these humans want to lie down
in the soil we shove

to bloom thrust our
waiting mouth into the sky
where I want you   to open my
struck meteor   we push inside one another
the rainbirds lush us   this circuit
of grasses   each cycle
alive   live   even trapped in their asphalt
along these lines of

their fault   too hot to touch
without tender   without some sense we are the
same   without

you   no I would remain   leap o Luna
your tresses your indecent iridescent tides
their cities could not disarm us
their cities could not

O Uncity

you have no right to die we
inside-out landfills
the garbage overgrown with sunflowers
lists to port becomes our
veranda vines creep
our backyard world where
the horns will scream until
the last car batteries bleed dry
the unknown she folds in my arms
whimpering in her shock you stand

in your rebar and concertina-wire disguise what I
loved so much gone
from your eyes each unsheathed and rattling *I
struck her when driving*
blind   look at our seas leaking oil into animal
form each of us
drilling our hard-case surmise under each
promise wilted
lay among my refuse
braid the Walmart bag into your brambled
thatch let's curl together
around her and listen to her final breath
so she knows we are
here for her

how could she uncity
let down her coiled copper hair at last
outside of herself she wails long distance
to her long-silenced pod

UNCITY,

lean

The temperature rises
and all that heat
from the cement reflects
not love
but the industry of love and looking
over your shoulder

Love at First Sight Hurl Your Chain-Mailed Fist into the Sky

i.

We take turns, try all night like hacks
to summon The Poet—unhindered
under the sails of sleep—we birth
black roses, and our bones may break but we never
find our own skin. Such
love: what my parents left in the fridge
between two jobs
and trading off who took night
school. The Snore returns—makes
love like water-
boarding. There is value in this desolation-family,
each hug its own funeral parlor, an open viewing of a
stranger among us. We reach
to hold hands just long enough for one of us
to retreat to the corner
of our cage. I eat
my father, fingers first
and then stoop to pick up his hat—reward
for long hours
watching me play in the public pool
or the moments bent gently teaching me how to read.
We fly Mom bloated & crucified
on her kite, the way she says she likes. In our sleep
the coffee is cold,
but we drink it all anyway so
no one else can.

ii.

One daffodil elbows its way
 through the cracks in an abandon-
    ed parking lot. We fold Mom, put her back on her shelf
after wearing her to work all day—the way
two women fight over what is torn between them.
Unbearable love. We re-
address the ax to The Poet's
flesh, bring our beaks down to her neck
to sip the necrotic rose and the skin-sacked pile of broken
bones we clamber over to hold hands
    in her cage, each page a sail for which
we paid her dearly in microwave pizza this
finite moment in which we must
all drown. All that I require
is that you are lovely when
it is our turn to be eaten. If so, we share an umbrella
    in the downpour of nothing
    but blue. Love at first sight, we throw our chain-
    mailed fist into
the. O love, to this tolling of your eyes.

Cutting the Mattress
with Our Dreams

i.

I smell the open jar the coyote
paw is still fresh—our passage was furnished
by this hope—a shivering hammer
on the dulcimer. Appalachian saints hooded

briskly walk backward into the ocean
we can forgo incense, essential oils, the false
monks drowning over the stamp of drum
machines; in all this meditation—I am

a coin
in the stripped mall
wishing well
wishing my son
will escape the roundabouts and the convenience
store tape-

          loop—how a freeway is like
a palindrome—be
the other
          merchandise that a water

store sells.

ii.

Cut the mattress, past the comfort control
top, mound the stuffing,
blood the spring, set the fire; when human
fat meets an accelerant, our only
predator. Open your door. Put your

hand inside the blind sunlion's mouth. Leave.
On the hill
          the coyote limps—hisses—it cannot
yip—smell its missing lower jaw I saved it

here in my jar.

Dawn in SubInlandia

My tightrope walker writes up another parking ticket
leaves it under my pillow—a somnambulant revolver
to the temple—my jester, she is
    handcuffed all the crow's feathers point
the same direction in flight—inward the sponge tucks

its dryness—the waiting nose of a cat—squeeze
    through this tight
gap in the door with my whisker—parallel park between
two moving vans. A ketchup bottle sweats. A Sheriff
sweats. At 6:45 the Sundowner Diner pants
from the heat coming off the concrete—inside the
screened-in patio, I sweat. The Honeycomb sweats.
                              Somewhere a dinner
plate screams
not again! A horned god rises above the irises and the
wheat—I lift the wind-
shield wiper—pick up the violation and the envelope—I
can't see her but she is
watching. And smiles.

The Land That Lies between Rancho Cucamonga and San Bernardina, California, at 7:38 a.m.:

City Scape I,

Wanted: Cheap
  tract homes that annex the field to
  glut the red wine for as little as possible in return as we sit
in the splinter of the wild—concrete
  shoe'd among the blooded
  and water-starved
grapevines. Around
  the corner—the scab-white plank
  wood and rebar scaffolding

belt the 7-11 and the Payday
  Advance—throw back the light
  from the gum-saturated walkway so that
workman can rebrand and repaint the building for
  the Fast-Evict-Law-Group
  that now sits behind red-rod-iron and concertina
wire-covered fences protecting a herd of stray
  impounded cars. Glut-skin
  algaes the mute

storm channel, makes its own advances, connecting
  Baldy to the L.A. basin like
  a low-slung freeway of stagnate
  traffic-scum. The deepest place our antifreeze pools is
in our groundwater. From there
  the Jimson Weed stalks from its fault-splinter
  bursting the concrete into fracture
nebulas. It is no secret
  that shadow lights up
  the raised places unpooled around our depressions.

Lost Tooth

The Lullybye We Had Missed from the Night Before

> *swaddled in her arms she*
> *sang goodnight sweet son*

last night we laughed—left work
Forgetting he was out there she and I plunged down the stairs
drenched
under a shared umbrella
my white car's wake
pushed the Cool
Ranch Doritos bag past the overfilled
mouth

> *swaddled in her arms she*
> *sang goodnight sweet son*

of the storm
drain
then they stole his seizure
medication, they stole
his blankets, "still alive!" big blue
eyes, that last time I talked with
him, I got him a Slurpee   now
it's morning and sober—we follow

> *swaddled in her arms she*
> *sang goodnight sweet son*

the big rig's wallow—its left
turn past the police car &   7-11—lights on
at his usual spot
a blue thrum   a sleeping bag draped over a body in
Rusty's wheelchair
next to the abandoned wing
of HMC² Holistic
medical practice.
swaddled in her arms she sang goodnight my sweet son.

The Clock Stopped.

2 scruffy
young men run down
Hospitality Lane holding
signs *Musicians on tour*
out of gas. They grab
crumpled dollar bills
thrown from passing cars like roses

A coffee cup
a prehistoric forest
crusted
salt sweat

A body hidden
waterlogged
in a sleeping bag
under overpass
blooms decay
the river lies

on its belly in the concrete reservoir, elephant grass explosion stuck in its craw. All working people need something personable to say when the boss walks by. For instance: Turner's Outdoorsman is selling more handguns than tents, or Target has closed its nursery.

Escape exile: the sun
                         a lone gunman
                         will consume
                         our inland empire.

Heatstrokeman talks   Your bootstraps   At Burger Mania
with his metronome.   a self-sufficient   50-year-old
At 295 bpm no one   boot kick scaffold. businessmen
can hear his music.   are arguing how
                                              best to stop
                                              immigration.

                    They think that we should all take
Heatstrokeman continues to wave   turns holding the gun
his arms in feverish circles   to the infant's head.
the rhythm of his metronome.

When Unexpectedly Confronted with *Nature Died with Sunflower*

i.

Yes I too see it now in the raw
beauty of the tract homes
all-grid

in both the vertical and the horizontal planes—people
dangle from
the cruciform phonelines

and those in power
flex the natural extension of the red-
wood and the pines

in their spines upright
lances of business
men and the dwellings where they stand or

sleep it takes courage
to see this contiguous
beauty

not the demarcation of human
and nature between which no line of distinction
can be drawn but between the non-gold

of the sunflower and the bold color of the sky
that entombs her.

ii.

Hold a pixilated stare
of the sunflower and the bold color of the sky
that entombs her in these rigid fields you thought straight-

jacketed her until the cracks appeared
in the paint of the wood-plank
fences sparked with superficial

erosion that showed you no
such regularities until the splinter entered your hand
split our dimensions or beings

but that these fields declare themselves open and full
in and of themselves queer
and each snared irregularity is a better signifier

for the purposeful decay of the old ways
like water
in the bottom of the glass

where the once-milk is suspended by its own nippled levity
caked into milk-white clay
and as unthinkably undrinkable

as the low-slung
crossbeam
of this cuneiform sky that looms over all of us.

And It Was Over]

```
              Recycling
            I crushed    the sunset from
                         the Crush
                  can    the hypochondriac
                         the syringe
         backpocketed    the fine-tuned shopping
                 list        every lover permits
      magic then leaves
        mythic—unseen            to further breath—eating
                         the other unsavory sub
             routines    the unrepentant cycle of clean
         sing trashday    the discography
                   of    the landfill
                         the self-mutilation of
              commute            casual
                  day    the sleeving of disposable
          coffee cups    the vetting of insurance carriers, !premiums
    !premiumsagonistic            board meetings
                         the pendulum over
             a pit of    the corpus economii
      my workshoes wet    the runners have holes where
         my feet feel    the wet concrete
                         the afternoons instanter upon
                         the images—framed well & focused
                         the condoms that captured vacations,
             family.    the closed albums neatly arranged in our
    domicile
            mausoleum    the tic tac toe of living together—we
    raced to blame
    someone            the white collar
```

                          the lab coats, but when y'all turned
around all I saw
were rhinosauri just
    like me. and someone had respun   the rent
aluminum into fine silicate bottling[the coming moonburn

Interview

i.

The hook and triangle
echo network of coat

hangers—they twitter—know
the way to cook marshmallows
gathered around the stone ring of executive
fire
we are caramelized
stuck to the deformed
handle their makeshift torch—hands sticky

with we assemblages
the twisted mobiles of the unassisted

school project made by our kids without us the night before
class the circling
kosmos of unnested
raptors—the flock of wolf-mates
spun fleece and wings nip
suspended by their twisted network of hangers
the botched street-side

removal of the child the way
some of us try to.

ii.

The removal of the child the way that
some of us try to

straighten what is seen as deformed mettle
to find someplace to put our clothes on
the hook and the triangle
this furry night before the next interview
the closed door laughing at our
need no matter which side of it
you are on
we are

to know shame

we must first know pride to know

pride we must first do unseen

work and those who think they know our worth with
their hands all over us
made too hot to touch
so they can distract themselves

with us
held over their fire—some
impaled meteor of sugary flesh
they cannot blow out to eat.

Late Night and Alone, at the Super 8:

Mary Watching the Roadway

i.

She stubs out the cherry on cracked whitewash railing,
but the smoke smell remains

so she can see you—untransforming thing, those days
lived inside your car, meshed in white lines through
which brake lights and halogens weave—all our roles

reversible. You will have nothing to eat but your own

song. You think of the things we abandon: one family,
at least, overtime, one home, at least—you don't stop
to watch me—sunburned, turn and descend into the
dry-stink of the flood control

channel—where the locust leaps into your grill to die.

ii.

You won't see me, lying still but finally alone in the wash among the Jimson—through my robe of chain-link, each wire diamond a snapshot thrown into a shoebox diorama

of unshown J-Doe. The black widow leaps across the webbed marble shower through her threads, to milk her unmoving orbs.

I see you sitting behind the wheel reeking of traffic— the tumble- weeds, burger wrapper, box spring, Big Gulp cup have blown themselves into the chain-link between us.

Slipping through the Knot I Saw Sunrise from My Knees

i.

under the quiet maidenhair trees we come
to the field to graze among these word-wolves
lick the warm round stones to pay for our dinner
while old mescal tongues cardboard papercuts on our lungs
there is no perfection without burning

leap into each other's mouth I concede
Stella Artois in her green bottles is not after all piss
4 photos walk into a sunrise at the top of our apartment stairs
throw them off the balcony
walk through the green glass together barefoot like roses
if we learn this language of barely touching
when I am the wolf tangled in your hair.

ii.

your belly grows my sleepless adoration
walks like a field of risen corpses among the midnight
sunflowers
by my engine's pistons I
come home for you with your long dark hair pulled
out in braids in the seat beside
kiss   the weeping between your thighs
the white balloon escapes from hell
surrenders crash   down gravity on   our backs
we bat it back into blue until our claws singsnag

its rubbery skin our scandalous   trash
      drains   like a waiting litter of kittens
      we will play love in the house of our stubborn laps
happily no escape her honey-silk spilt all over me
                      throws her wolf mane back into the stars.

      She smiles down, says it's too late.
                              You are part of it now.

ABOUT *the* AUTHOR

Michael Cooper

is an Inland Empire poet, PoetrIE member, MFA student, veteran, and father of two great sons: Markus & Jonathan. His work is in *Tin Cannon*, *The Pacific Review*, *The Chaffey Review*, *The Coil*, *The Camel Saloon*, *The Los Angeles Review*, *H-NGM-N*, *The Berkeley Review*, *The Portland Review*, *The Sky Is a Free Country: The Luminaire Award Anthology Vol. 1*, and other fine (but wild) publications. Michael would like to make you aware that the splash zone includes the first eleven rows.

The AUTHOR WISHES *to* THANK:

Cindy Rinne, Tim Hatch, and Eric "T.R.U.E." De-Vaughnn for reading this manuscript and giving me great feedback, and for the push to put one foot in front of the other.

George! Your timely intervention and publication of "Midnight Firetruck" probably saved this book.

Terra, Markus, Jonathan, the pups, and the cat-who-thinks-he-is-a pup. You are my rock.

Grider! From kindergarten to old age, may we always raise a glass to life and art.

Laurie, for giving me shelter when things went wrong, and for creating a wonderful daughter and family.

The CSUSB crew and all the people who both tolerated me and cajoled me into being a better human.

Leah, and Alternating Current, for taking the time to help me hone and deploy this book.

A special thanks to Arianna Basco, who encouraged me to keep going when I was scarred and the world was dark, and Gina Duran for being a light and a wonder in this dread-cold Inland Empire.

ACKNOWLEDGMENTS

"Midnight Firetruck," "Every Love Song I Sing to Myself," "Art Lesson I," "History Lesson I," and "History Lesson II" were previously published in *The Oklahoma Review*.

"Playground III," "Playground IV," "Playground V," and "A Prayer for the Horned-Ones III" were previously published in different versions in *Atlas and Alice*.

"A Prayer for the Horned-Ones I" and "A Prayer for the Horned-Ones II" were previously published in *Elohi Gadugi Journal*.

"The Return Commute through the Street-Fight I Am Transmuted to You through Sound" and "The Lullybye We Had Missed from the Night Before" were previously published in different versions in *The Pacific Review*.

"Our Lives Depend on Knowing What to Wear, What to Say," "To Some the Highway Is Just a High-Power Rifle," "But I Always Thought That I'd See You Again," "No 'They,' We Are All One Organism Of," and "O Uncity" were previously published in different versions in *Sparkle and Blink*.

"My Friend Ended Himself the Grass Grows" was previously published in a different version in *Sundog Lit*.

"Cutting the Mattress with Our Dreams" was previously published in *The Los Angeles Review*.

"When Unexpectedly Confronted with *Nature Died with Sunflower*" was previously published in *The Collapsar*.

"Slipping through the Knot I Saw Sunrise from My Knees" was previously published in *Sand Canyon Review*.

COLOPHON

The edition you are holding is the First Edition of this publication.

The distorted title font is El Tercer Hombre, created by Bumbayo Font Fabrik. The cursive title font is Hey October, created by Khurasan. The sans serif subtitle font on the cover is Din, created by Albert-Jan Pool. All other text is Athelas, created by José Scaglione and Veronika Burian. The Alternating Current Press logo is Portmanteau, created by JLH Fonts. All fonts used with permission; all rights reserved.

Cover artwork created by Leah Angstman and Mad Max. The Alternating Current lightbulb logo was created by Leah Angstman, ©2013, 2021 Alternating Current. All artwork used with permission; all rights reserved.

All material used with permission; all rights reserved.

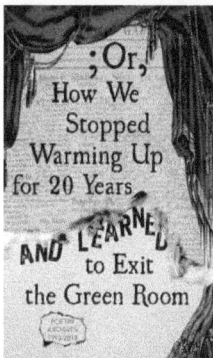

alternatingcurrentarts.com